THE COMPLETE GUIDE TO
EXTREME WEATHER

Sandy Creek
NEW YORK

An Imprint of Sterling Publishing Co., Inc.
1166 Avenue of the Americas
New York, NY 10036

ISBN: 978-1-4351-6354-6

Manufactured in Guangdong, China
Lot #:
2   4   6   8   10   9   7   5   3
03/18

www.sterlingpublishing.com

THE COMPLETE GUIDE TO
EXTREME
WEATHER

LOUISE SPILSBURY AND ANNA CLAYBOURNE

Sandy Creek
NEW YORK

CONTENTS

WEATHER EXTREMES

Humans have figured out how to control many things. They farm crops and animals, reshape the land, and build giant towers and bridges. However, one thing they have little control over is the world's weather. There is not much people can do to stop a downpour, prevent a lightning strike, or change the path of a fast, deadly, roaring hurricane. Human beings are at the weather's mercy.

A summer thunderstorm puts on a stunning display of lightning over Beirut, Lebanon.

When Weather Turns Wild

Weather does not always cause problems. Sometimes, the weather is perfect and, other times, it is annoying. Occasionally, extreme and scary weather conditions come along. Powerful winds, lightning strikes, **heat waves**, and ice storms can be dangerous and deadly. Extreme weather can lead to other disasters too, such as floods, **landslides**, traffic accidents, and electricity blackouts.

A "supercell" storm cloud, like this one, can create deadly tornadoes.

World Weather

The same changes in the atmosphere that determine ordinary weather cause extreme weather. Some types of extreme weather happen only in certain places on the planet, such as blizzards that happen only in the coldest areas. Some types of extreme weather, such as lightning, can happen anywhere.

Debris blocks a road after Typhoon Soudelor, which affected parts of China and Taiwan in 2015.

LIGHTNING FACT

There are about 2,000 thunderstorms per minute on Earth. The Indonesian island of Java has thunderstorms on about 220 days of every year.

EARTH'S ATMOSPHERE

Weather is what's going on in the atmosphere—the thin layer of gases around Earth. Water, air, and the temperature in the atmosphere affect the weather. The air contains water in the form of **water vapor**, clouds, or **fog**. Air moving around the planet makes wind. Sunshine, the time of year, and where the wind has come from all affect the temperature.

The atmosphere is only 435 miles deep and is held around Earth by the force of **gravity**.

EXOSPHERE
435–6,214 miles
above Earth's surface

THERMOSPHERE
50–435 miles
above Earth's surface

MESOSPHERE
31–50 miles
above Earth's surface

STRATOSPHERE
7.5–31 miles
above Earth's surface

TROPOSPHERE
0-7.5 miles
above Earth's surface

Five Layers of Gases

The atmosphere has five layers. The thickest layer, called the troposphere, is closest to Earth. Above the troposphere is the stratosphere. This is where jets often fly. Above the stratosphere is the mesosphere, and then the thermosphere, where spacecraft **orbit** Earth. The exosphere is the final layer that fades into space.

Water, air, and changing temperatures in Earth's lower atmosphere create the weather on Earth.

The higher you go in the atmosphere, the thinner the air becomes and the harder it is to breathe.

Air in the Troposphere

The troposphere is where most of Earth's weather happens. It contains 90 percent of all the air in Earth's atmosphere. The air can heat up, cool down, and move around. It also has a pushing force, called air pressure.

Water in the Troposphere

The troposphere also contains water in the form of a gas called water vapor. Changing temperatures change the state of this water vapor. When the temperature cools, water vapor **condenses** and collects into water droplets, to form clouds.

LIGHTNING FACT

Most **meteors** do not crash-land on Earth because they burn up when they hit the mesosphere. When they do make it through to Earth, they are called meteorites.

AIR PRESSURE

The atmosphere pushes down on Earth, creating air pressure. The air may not seem very heavy but because the atmosphere is about 62 miles deep, there is a huge weight of air above us. It presses in and down on us all the time, from all around. The reason people do not feel air pressure squashing them is because they are used to it.

Differences in atmospheric pressure cause the wind that blows in from the oceans.

High Pressure

High pressure happens when air is sinking toward the ground from higher in the atmosphere. The sinking air spreads out slowly, so it is less windy. High pressure usually means calm, settled weather, which can be warm or cool.

On weather maps, lines called isobars show pressure. Highs and lows appear as groups of circles.

H 1033
1028
1024
20
L 989
996
1008
1004
000
2

Low Pressure

Areas of low pressure, sometimes called "lows," happen where warmer, lighter air is rising. As the air rises and cools, the water in it forms clouds. The rising air also causes wind as cooler air rushes in. Low pressure usually results in unsettled, cloudy, or rainy weather.

Low pressure can create clouds that bring rainy weather.

Lowest in the Atmosphere

The lowest air pressure in the atmosphere is found in the middle of hurricanes, cyclones, and tornadoes. Weather forecasters measure pressure in millibars (mb). The average pressure on Earth's surface is about 1013 mb. In 2005, Hurricane Wilma recorded pressure of 882 mb.

Tornadoes, like this one on the American plains, are formed when high-pressure air and low-pressure air interact.

LIGHTNING FACT

Normal air pressure is like a weight of 14.7 pounds per square inch pushing down on a person's body.

WEATHER FRONTS

Cold air

Weather forecasters often talk about "fronts." A weather front is a dividing line between two different blocks, or masses, of air. One air mass may be cold and dry, while another could be warm and damp. Scientists use the name "front" to compare the two air masses battling against each other with two armies fighting at the frontline in a war.

This bank of cloud is a cold front pushing against a mass of warm air.

Warm Fronts

A warm front is the edge of a mass of warm air pushing against a mass of colder air. The warm air gradually rises above the mass of cold air. As it rises and cools, it forms clouds. That is why warm fronts often bring rain and drizzle.

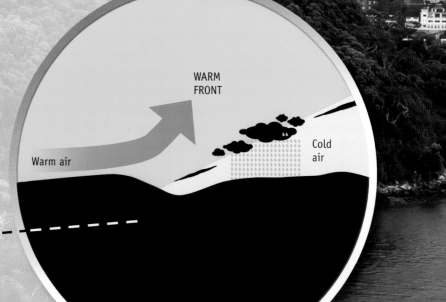

WARM FRONT

Warm air

Cold air

This is how warm fronts work

Cold Fronts

A cold front is where a mass of cold air meets a mass of warmer air. The cold air blows beneath the mass of warm air, forcing the warm air to rise more quickly. The warm air then forms thick cumulonimbus clouds, which bring heavy rain and strong winds.

Cold fronts can cause thick cumulonimbus clouds that bring heavy rain.

LIGHTNING FACT

On weather maps, cold fronts are shown as blue lines with triangles. Warm fronts are shown as red lines with semicircles.

12

016

1025
H

1024

A Change in Temperature

Weather fronts can cause stormy and cloudy weather, but they are known for the change in temperature that they bring. After a warm front has passed, the temperature becomes warmer. A spell of cold and dry weather usually follows a cold front.

THE POWER OF THE SUN

Most of our planet's weather is caused by something far away from Earth: the Sun. Besides giving us bright, sunny days, the Sun heats up Earth and the air around it. The heat makes the air move, causing wind and weather fronts. It also makes water from the oceans, rivers, lakes, and plants **evaporate** into the air, which leads to rain and snow.

The Sun provides all the light and heat that powers Earth's weather.

A Vast Ball of Gas

The Sun is a star—a huge ball of burning gas that creates vast amounts of heat and light energy. The temperature at the Sun's core (center) is about 30 million degrees Fahrenheit. Heat flows from the core to the surface of the Sun and then across space to Earth.

LIGHTNING FACT

The surface of the Sun has its own weather, including tornadoes.

Light from the Sun can damage eyes, so people should wear sunglasses when it's sunny.

Invisible Rays

The light energy released by the Sun can be seen, but a lot of the energy given off by Earth's nearest star is invisible. The **infrared** rays that heat Earth cannot be seen, and neither can the **ultraviolet** (UV) rays that can cause sunburn.

Heat from the Sun

As the Sun shines on Earth, it warms up Earth's surface. It is close enough for its heat to spread into the troposphere—the layer of air closest to Earth (see pages 8–9).

15

THE GREENHOUSE EFFECT

Most of the heat from the Sun that travels to Earth is **reflected** into space by its atmosphere. Some of the heat that gets through bounces off Earth's surface back into space. However, gases in the atmosphere trap some heat in the sky. These gases act like a blanket, keeping Earth warm. This is called the greenhouse effect because the gases trap warmth, like glass in a greenhouse.

Low, thick clouds in the troposphere reflect some of the Sun's light and heat into space, cooling Earth's surface.

LIGHTNING FACT

Less than one-millionth of the energy released by the Sun reaches Earth's surface.

Life on Earth

Without the greenhouse effect, there would be no life on Earth. The Sun's energy makes Earth the right temperature for living things to survive. It is the right temperature for water to exist in its liquid form. Living things need liquid water to survive.

Distance Matters

The Sun and Earth are 93 million miles apart. The Sun is just the right distance from Earth. If it were closer to the Sun, all the water would boil and evaporate into gas. Farther away, and all the water would be ice.

Greenhouse gases in the atmosphere trap some heat to keep Earth warm.

Sun

Atmosphere

Some heat from the Sun reflects off Earth's surface and escapes into space.

Some of the heat that reflects off Earth's surface is trapped by greenhouse gases in the atmosphere.

Icy Mountaintops

High mountaintops are very cold because the heat radiated from the ground cools as it rises up into the air. The air becomes thinner and more spread out higher in the troposphere, and the air pressure is lower. Air with a lower pressure also has a lower temperature, which makes the weather cooler.

Ice caps and glaciers reflect sunshine.

17

DAYS AND SEASONS

In most parts of the world, the weather changes according to the seasons. Some places have a warm summer and a cold winter. Other places have a rainy season and a dry season. The weather also becomes colder as day turns to night. Seasons and days happen because of the way Earth revolves around the Sun.

Spinning Earth

On Earth, there is day and night because Earth is spinning on its axis. The axis is an imaginary line passing through Earth's North and South Poles. Earth spins around once every 24 hours. Each day, a person's home moves into the sunlight, then out of it, so it experiences day and night.

Spring in northern hemisphere. Fall in southern hemisphere.

N

S

N

S

Summer in northern hemisphere. Winter in southern hemisphere.

LIGHTNING FACT

Scientists think Earth is tilted because another planet crashed into it billions of years ago.

A Year on Earth

Earth and the other planets follow a path, called an orbit, around the Sun. Earth's orbit is like a squashed circle. It takes one year (365 and one-quarter days) for Earth to make a complete orbit of the Sun, and to return to where it started.

Winter in northern hemisphere.
Summer in southern hemisphere.

N

S

Earth is the third planet from the Sun.

N

Fall in northern hemisphere.
Spring in southern hemisphere.

Summer and Winter

Earth is slightly tilted, so for part of the year, the northern **hemisphere** leans toward the Sun. As Earth moves around, the southern hemisphere leans toward the Sun. It is summer in the hemisphere that is leaning toward the Sun, and it is winter in the other hemisphere.

When it is winter in Russia and Canada, it is summer in Australia.

WET AND DRY SEASONS

While some regions of Earth have four seasons a year, others have just two: one rainy and one dry. In regions around the **equator**, it is so hot that water evaporates quickly. It forms a band of clouds. As Earth moves and tilts toward and away from the Sun, this band of clouds moves north and south, creating alternating wet and dry seasons.

The hot, dry season makes places in the tropics, like Mahe island in the Seychelles, popular beach destinations.

The Tropics

The tropics are the regions on either side of the equator. In the tropics south of the equator, the rainy season occurs between October and March. At the same time, the tropics north of the equator experience a dry season. In the tropics north of the equator, the rainy season occurs between April and September.

In the tropics south of the equator, the dry season is between April and September.

Changing Seasons

In the tropics, the seasons do not change suddenly. There is a gradual change from wet to dry. Toward the end of a dry season, when the moisture in the air starts to build up, the air feels humid. This **humidity** increases as clouds grow bigger, until eventually, the rains start to fall.

Wet or Dry?

In the dry season, it is very hot in the tropics and there is very little rain. The earth can dry up and plants may die. In the rainy season, there can be rain all day. The rainy season often brings thunder and lightning, too.

The clouds that bring wet seasons to places such as Thailand are known as the tropical rain belt.

LIGHTNING FACT

A dry season month is a month when average rainfall is below 2.4 inches.

LAND AND SEA

When the Sun shines on land, the land heats up quickly, but it also loses heat quickly. Water, however, heats up slowly. It takes a huge amount of energy from the Sun to warm up the sea. Once it is warm, it cools down slowly, so the sea acts like a big storage tank for the Sun's heat.

Clouds form over a Pacific Ocean island as warm air rises and cools.

Sizzling or Freezing Inland

Far from the sea, temperatures can be more extreme. When it is sunny, the Sun heats up the land fast. The land warms up the air above it, leading to very hot weather. At night, and in winter, the heat is lost quickly. The temperature drops fast, and winters can be freezing.

LIGHTNING FACT

Most of the world's biggest cities are on coasts, where the climate is **temperate**.

People often head to the coast in summer to cool down. This crowded beach is on the shore of Lake Michigan.

Cool and Warm Coasts

Coastal areas tend to have less extreme temperatures than inland areas. In summer, the sea takes heat from the land, so the land near the sea becomes fairly cool. In winter, the sea stores heat from the Sun collected over summer, and warms the coast.

Sea Breeze

At the coast, it is often quite windy. This is because the warm land heats up the air above it, and the air gets lighter and rises. Cool air over the sea then rushes in to take its place, making wind.

Windsurfers take advantage of strong sea breezes.

23

BOILING HOT

Most people call hot, sunny weather "good" weather, but it can get too hot. Sometimes, it even feels as if it is boiling hot. Hot weather is never actually boiling, but how hot a place gets depends on where it is. Earth is **spherical** and the Sun's rays travel in straight lines. They hit the equator at a right angle, so it is hottest there.

Areas along the equator get the biggest share of the Sun's energy.

Hottest Weather Ever

The hottest weather in history was recorded on July 10, 1913, in Death Valley, which is part of the Mojave Desert in California. The temperature there was 134 degrees Fahrenheit. Deserts are hot because there are few clouds or trees to block the Sun, and bare sand and rock soak up the Sun's heat.

The Hottest Place

Dallol in Ethiopia, Africa, holds the record for being the hottest place in which people have lived. It has an average daily maximum temperature of 94 degrees Fahrenheit. Today, no one lives in Dallol.

Death Valley is incredibly hot because it has a deep bowl shape. The air inside the bowl heats up and cannot spread out.

The volcanic landscape of Dallol, Ethiopia, is made up of acid ponds and salt desert plains.

LIGHTNING FACT

The hottest year on record in the United States was 2014. In that year, temperatures were 100 degrees Fahrenheit for ten or more days.

HEAT WAVES AND HEAT ISLANDS

In a heat wave, the weather is much hotter than usual, and the hot weather lasts for longer than expected for the time of year. Heat waves are caused by a mass of sinking air, which presses down and traps the Sun's heat near Earth's surface. This makes the ground and the air above it hotter and hotter. Heat waves can be very uncomfortable. They can even cause death.

Heat Wave Horror

Besides being hot, the air in a heat wave is often humid. This means that it holds a lot of water. People perspire to cool down, but in humid weather, it is harder for sweat to evaporate into the air. People easily become too hot and **dehydrated**, and this can be very dangerous.

Heat Islands

If a town or city is hotter than the surrounding countryside, it is said to be a heat island. Cities can become heat islands because their bricks, concrete, and asphalt heat up in the Sun. Machines, lights, cars, and heating systems all heat up cities even more.

Heat islands show up in winter. This city's snow is melting faster than the snow in the surrounding fields.

Teenagers try to escape from the summer heat in a fountain in Krakow, Poland.

LIGHTNING FACT

A heat wave makes the air so hot that it can make train tracks bend.

What to Do in a Heat Wave

To stay safe in a heat wave, people should avoid going outside in the heat of the day, around lunchtime. They should take cool showers if they feel too hot, and drink plenty of water. It can also help to eat cold foods like salads and to avoid doing anything too strenuous.

People in Montreal, Canada, keep cool during a heat wave by jumping into the city's fountains.

HEAT WAVE CASE STUDIES

These are some of the worst heat waves that have happened around the world in recent history.

People cool off in the fountains in front of the Eiffel Tower, in Paris, France, during a 2012 heat wave.

France 2003

The heat wave in Europe in 2003 affected France very badly. More than 15,000 people died, many of them elderly. So many died that there was not enough space in French mortuaries to store the bodies, so special mortuaries were set up in refrigeration vehicles.

United States 2006

During July 2006, a sweltering heat wave hit most of the United States. Air temperatures soared beyond 100 degrees Fahrenheit. The heat killed at least 126 people. American farmers faced major crop loss, and power companies struggled to keep up with electricity demands.

In the summer of 2010, a heat wave broke all Russian records. In Moscow, the daytime temperatures reached 101 degrees Fahrenheit. More than 50,000 people died, and the high temperatures destroyed a substantial amount of that year's wheat harvest.

MOSCOW 2010

Boys escape the heat in the Russian capital, Moscow, during the heat wave of 2010.

India 2015

It is not unusual for India to be hot but, in 2015, India was struck by one of the world's worst ever heat waves. For much of May that year, parts of India reached temperatures of 110 degrees Fahrenheit. In the capital city, New Delhi, it was hot enough to melt pavements. The heat wave killed at least 2,300 people.

Locals use umbrellas to keep cool in Calcutta, India, during the heat wave of 2015.

29

DRY AS A BONE

Deserts are the driest parts of the world. A non-desert area, such as the United Kingdom or New Zealand, receives more than 40 inches of rainfall in an average year. Deserts receive less than one-quarter of that—up to 10 inches and, sometimes, as little as 0.4 inches.

What Makes a Desert?

Some deserts, such as the Gobi in Asia, are in the middle of large areas of land, far from the seas where most clouds form. Others, such as the Namib in southern Africa, are near the sea, but strong winds blow the damp sea air away, leaving the desert dry.

The Atacama Desert, northern Chile.

LIGHTNING FACT

The Atacama Desert in South America is the driest place in the world. Parts of it have not had any rain in decades.

The Rain Shadow Effect

Mountains can cause desert conditions in the areas behind them—their rain shadows. As clouds blow toward the mountains, they rise up the slopes and become colder. This makes the water in them fall as rain. The clouds are used up, so the areas beyond the mountains rarely receive rain.

Prevailing winds have lost their moisture on the windward side of mountains in Fuerteventura, Canary Islands, Spain, leaving this side dry.

The Antarctic continent is called a cold desert because there is no liquid water there.

Cold Deserts

There are hot deserts and cold deserts. Antarctica is very dry because, although it is covered in water, the water is frozen into ice and snow, and not much rain falls each year. This makes Antarctica a cold desert.

DROUGHTS

A drought happens when a place that normally gets rain has a period of unusually dry weather. Some places have short droughts, when high-pressure weather systems mean no rain falls for a few weeks. The droughts end when low-pressure weather systems carrying rain blow into the area. In some places, high-pressure systems hang around for months or even years, and these droughts can have devastating effects.

Where Droughts Happen

Short droughts can happen anywhere. The worst droughts happen in places with hot, dry climates. The Sahel area of northern Africa, the western United States, and parts of China have all had terrible droughts.

Effects of Droughts

In places that have short droughts, people may have to reduce the water they use for some time. Governments turn off fountains, people water their backyards with wastewater, and they stop taking full baths until the drought is over.

In a severe drought, there may not be enough water to go around.

Life on Earth relies on water, so droughts can be disastrous.

Droughts kill crops that people need.

Famine

In places with severe droughts, the effects can be deadly. Droughts cause the land to dry out, so plants cannot grow. Without plants to eat, animals die. In poorer countries where many people cannot buy the food they need, droughts can lead to famines, causing millions of people to starve.

LIGHTNING FACT

Only 0.003 percent of water on Earth is freshwater available for human consumption.

DROUGHT CASE STUDIES

These are some of the worst droughts in recent history.

Australia 2003–2009

From about 2003 to 2009, Australia suffered a long drought known as the Millennium Drought or the "Big Dry." Lakes dried up and forests that once lined some of the continent's rivers died. Dams were reduced to 25 percent capacity. Crops died and farmers had to sell off their livestock.

Weather researchers now predict that droughts affect Australia about every 18 years.

A drought in China dried out this farmer's field.

China 2014

In 2014, China suffered its worst drought in more than 50 years. The worst-hit areas included the region known as China's breadbasket, which grows much of the country's corn, wheat, and soybeans. Water levels were so low that millions of people did not have enough drinking water.

Getting enough water is often a daily struggle in Ethiopia, but in times of drought, it is impossible.

Horn of Africa 2011

Between 50,000 and 100,000 people, more than half of them children under five, died in the drought that hit Somalia, Ethiopia, and Kenya in the Horn of Africa in 2011. When the losses of livestock and crops are counted, this drought caused a food crisis for a total of 13 million people.

Reservoirs ran low in California during the drought of 2015.

California 2015

In 2015, the state of California suffered its fourth summer of drought. **Reservoirs** dried up, water restrictions were imposed, and people were asked to let their lawns die. To prevent future water shortages, new desalination projects, which make freshwater from seawater, are being encouraged.

WILDFIRES

A wildfire is when an area of scrubland, forest, or bush catches fire, and flames spread very quickly and uncontrollably over a wide region. A wildfire can rage for days or weeks and can cause terrible damage to plants, wildlife, property, and people. Wildfires usually happen during hot, dry seasons and during times of drought.

How Wildfires Start

When plants dry up in the heat, they catch fire more easily. Wildfires may be started by a flash of lightning. More often, wildfires are started accidentally when people drop cigarette stubs or fail to put out campfires properly.

Forest fires and wind completely destroyed forests during a severe drought in southern Ukraine.

Putting Out Wildfires

Wildfires spread because burning embers blow from plant to plant. Firefighters cut down lines of trees to make firebreaks to stop the fire from spreading. They drop water or **chemicals** from aircraft to put out fires.

Winds blow flames between trees and increase the speed at which a forest fire spreads.

Fire Whirls

Wildfires can sometimes create fire whirls or fire devils, which look like red tornadoes. Hot, dry air rising rapidly from the ground causes fire devils. As the hot air spins upward, it picks up burning embers, ash, hot gases, and burning debris, creating a terrifying tower of flames.

To avoid starting a wildfire, campers should always properly extinguish campfires before they leave.

WILDFIRE CASE STUDIES

Here are some of the most dramatic wildfires that have occurred in recent years.

In summer 2007, forest fires in Greece killed 84 people and burned 670,000 acres of forests and fields. The fires burned from June to September but were deadliest in August, when they killed 67 people. The fires were stopped as they reached the outskirts of Athens, Greece's capital city.

Greece 2007

In 2007, fires on Mount Parnitha could be seen 18 miles away in Greece's capital city, Athens.

Australia 2009

On Saturday February 8, 2009, after weeks of drought and heat, Australia experienced its worst recorded fires in history. The day became known as Black Saturday—173 people died and 5,000 were injured. More than 2,000 homes were destroyed, many animals were killed, and vast areas of land were burned.

Forest damage near Beechworth, Victoria, after the 2009 Black Saturday bushfires in Australia.

Heat and drought regularly cause wildfires in California, but those in 2014 were some of the most destructive. By the end of the year, there had been 5,620 wildfires, which burned at least 631,434 acres of land. The wildfires caused a total of 146 injuries and killed two people.

Firefighters work to control a large wildfire that grew out of control in the hills above Glendora, California, in 2014.

In 2015, thousands of forest fires raged across the islands of Indonesia. Some burned for months. The fires caused thick smoke that is likely to cause the premature deaths of more than 100,000 people. Large areas of forest, where endangered species such as orangutans live, were destroyed.

In 2015, smoke from the fires burning across Indonesia filled cities as far away as Thailand with smoke.

WILD WIND

People very seldom notice the air that is all around them, especially when they are indoors. However, they do notice it when it starts to move. Moving air creates wind. Wind can blow hats off heads and turn umbrellas inside out. When it is strong, it can flatten houses, blow down trees, and flip vehicles.

This powerful windstorm on the island of Fiji, in the South Pacific Ocean, is blasting the trees sideways.

The Sun's energy makes the air move by heating it.

Cooler air moves in to take warm air's place

Wind

Warm air rises

What Makes Wind?

Heat from the Sun creates wind. First, sunshine heats up the land. The hot land then heats up the air above it. This warm air spreads out and becomes lighter. As it becomes lighter, it also rises, allowing colder, heavier air from cooler areas to rush in as wind.

LIGHTNING FACT

The fastest winds in the world are found inside tornadoes.

Prevailing Winds

The prevailing wind is the most frequent wind direction a location experiences. Sometimes, trees will grow leaning over to one side. The prevailing wind causes this, pushing the tree harder on one side than the other.

A windblown tree in Yorkshire, England

When the kite catches the wind, the surfer, who is holding on to the kite, is carried across the water.

Sun and Wind

The Sun heats up some parts of Earth more than others. Land heats up more than sea, and areas near the equator heat up more than areas near the poles. This means winds are constantly blowing from one place to another.

41

WINDS OF THE WORLD

Local weather may change from day to day, but around the globe, winds tend to follow a pattern. Winds circulate the globe as a result of Earth's spinning and the heat energy from the Sun. If Earth did not rotate, winds would blow in a straight line, from the poles to the equator. The spinning Earth bends the winds.

Cool air

Warm air

Cell

Air systems called cells exist all over the planet.

Cells

Warm, rising air creates air systems called **cells**. In one part of a cell, the air rises into the troposphere. It moves far away, then sinks in another area, moving in a giant loop.

The Trade Winds

The trade winds, shown in red, helped
sailors cross from Europe to the Caribbean.
The westerlies, shown in green, helped
them sail home again. The doldrums
(purple band) is an area of light winds.
Sailing ships crossing the doldrums were
sometimes at a standstill for days.

This map shows the location
of the trade winds.

Sails are designed
to catch the wind
and to use its
energy to move
ships forward.

Jet Streams

Jet streams are rivers of fast-moving winds
that move weather systems around the world.
Jet streams flow high in the troposphere
5.6 to 10 miles above Earth's surface.
A jet stream usually marks the boundary
between cold polar air to its north,
and warmer air to its south.

By flying with the flow of
a jet stream, aircraft can cut
flight times and save fuel

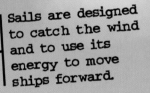

LIGHTNING FACT

Jet streams can reach speeds
of 200 miles per hour.

43

MONSOONS

From May each year, monsoon winds bring heavy rain and storms to countries such as India, Bangladesh, Nepal, Pakistan, and Sri Lanka. These monsoon rains can be a relief to people in places affected by drought, and many communities celebrate their arrival. However, heavy monsoon rains can also flood towns and villages, and destroy fields of crops.

Boys enjoy the newly flooded streets during monsoon season in Calcutta, India, in 2015.

How Monsoon Winds Work

As warm air rises over the hot land in summer in South and Southeast Asia, cool, moist air from the ocean blows in to fill the space left behind, bringing rain. Later, when the land cools, the winds change direction and blow from land to sea, and the weather on land is dry again.

LIGHTNING FACT

India receives three-quarters of its total annual rainfall between June and September.

When Monsoons Happen

Monsoons blow from the southwest between May and September, bringing rain and a wet monsoon season. They blow from the northeast between October and April, during the dry monsoon season. Before monsoon rains come, temperatures can become hot and humid.

Men push a car through the flooded streets of Lahore, Pakistan, in 2011.

The Monsoon in India

Monsoon rains account for around 80 percent of India's total annual rainfall. During the monsoon season every June and July, parts of the country become the wettest places in the world. These rains are vital for India's farmers.

Women pick tea leaves in India. Monsoon winds provide rain for the crops.

STORMS

When a storm is predicted in a weather forecast, it usually means some kind of extreme or bad weather. Most storms combine strong winds with other kinds of severe weather, such as heavy rain, thunder and lightning, or snow. Storms often occur in summer, when there is a lot of heat and humidity.

Storms at Douro harbor in Portugal can bring wind gusts that reach speeds of 93 miles per hour.

These dark clouds are a sign that a large storm is on its way.

What Causes a Storm?

Wind blows from areas of high pressure toward areas of low pressure. If a high-pressure area and a low-pressure area are very close, or if the pressure difference is very great, strong winds are created. If there is a lot of water in the air, dark clouds form and produce heavy rain.

Swirling Storms

As a result of the way Earth spins, winds swirl in a spiral as they move into a low-pressure area. Hurricanes and tornadoes are made of super-fast, spiraling winds. Storms can also move across a region, leaving a trail of destruction behind them.

There are several different kinds of storms, including ice storms like this one.

LIGHTNING FACT

Fear of thunder and lightning by people or animals is called astraphobia.

THUNDER AND LIGHTNING

Thunderstorms, or electric storms, happen when a lot of warm, wet air rises quickly into the sky. As the warm air cools, it piles up into tall thunderclouds. Thunderclouds can produce lightning, heavy rain, hail, or snow.

LIGHTNING FACT

The electrical energy in a flash of lightning could toast 100,000 slices of bread!

A flash of forked lightning lights up a meadow of hay bales.

How Lightning Happens

Thunderclouds reach high into the atmosphere, where it is so cold that the water droplets in the clouds freeze into ice crystals and hailstones. These bump and rub against each other, causing static electricity to build up—just as it does when a balloon is rubbed against a sweater. The electrical energy in the thundercloud is released as giant sparks, called lightning.

Lightning Strikes

Strikes happen about 50 times a second. **Global warming** is increasing this rate, as more warm air produces more thunderstorms. Lightning that jumps between a cloud and the ground is called forked lightning. If it jumps from one part of a cloud to another, it is called sheet lightning. Lightning is constantly striking Earth somewhere.

Thunderclaps

Thunder is the sound of lightning. A lightning flash heats up the air around it, making it explode. This creates a shock wave that is heard as a loud crash or rumble. Light travels much faster than sound, so the lightning flash is seen before the thunder is heard.

What to Do in a Thunderstorm

A lightning spark takes the shortest path it can between the cloud and the ground, so it usually strikes tall things. If people are ever caught in a thunderstorm, they should never shelter under a tree or near a hilltop, and should never wave an umbrella, golf club, or other metal object in the air.

Trees work like lightning rods on the top of a building, conducting electrical charges from the clouds.

49

HURRICANES, TYPHOONS, AND CYCLONES

Tropical cyclones have different names depending on where they form. If they start in the Atlantic or eastern Pacific Ocean, they are called hurricanes. If they form in the northwestern Pacific Ocean, they are called typhoons, and if they start in the southwestern Pacific or Indian Ocean, they are known as cyclones. They are among the most powerful storms of all.

How Hurricanes Work

Hurricanes form over warm, tropical oceans. Heat from the Sun warms the water so it evaporates into the air. As moist air heats up and rises, the water in the air forms a mass of heavy rainclouds. Cooler air moves in to replace the rising air, swirling in a spiral because of the way the Earth rotates.

A typical hurricane measures around 280 miles wide.

Eye

Warm air rising

Cool air sinking

Eyewall

Eye of the Hurricane

In a hurricane, air is mostly rising. However, right in the middle, the air sinks, creating a cloud-free spot called the "eye" of the storm. The bank of clouds around the eye, called the "eyewall," is the windiest, wettest part of the storm. The weather in the eye itself is much calmer.

Hurricane eye

Weather forecasters sometimes give tropical cyclones their own names. This **satellite** image shows Hurricane Felix from 2007. The gap in the middle is the eye of the hurricane.

Hurricane Fran, which formed in the Atlantic Ocean, is seen here from above, about to make landfall in Florida.

LIGHTNING FACT

Hurricanes can grow to be 560 miles wide in just a few days.

More on the Way?

For a hurricane to form, the temperature of the surface of the sea needs to be about 79 degrees Fahrenheit or higher. Earth's climate is warming up (see pages 124–125). This means seas will reach the trigger temperature more often, so in the future, there will probably be more hurricanes across the world.

HURRICANE AND CYCLONE CASE STUDIES

Hurricanes and cyclones happen every year. These are some of the worst in recent history.

Houses in Cancun, Mexico, destroyed by a hurricane.

Hurricane Odile, Mexico 2014

When Hurricane Odile roared into Mexico's Baja California Peninsula in September 2014, it toppled trees, power lines, and signs, and smashed the fronts of hotel resorts. Flying glass injured people as hotel windows were smashed and cars were wrecked.

Hurricane Sandy, North America 2012

Hurricane Sandy was one of the most devastating hurricanes of recent years, tearing through the Caribbean and North America in October 2012. Its strong winds and heavy rain caused floods, cut off power, and destroyed homes from Jamaica to Ontario, Canada.

Cyclone Yasi, Australia 2011

In February 2011, Cyclone Yasi became one of the biggest cyclones to hit Australia in the country's history. Yasi had a 404-mile-long storm front and winds up to 177 miles per hour. It smashed homes, shredded crops, and destroyed **marinas** and island resorts.

Volunteers clean up the debris caused by cyclone damage in Brisbane, Australia, in 2011.

Cyclone Pam, South Pacific 2015

Cyclone Pam was one of the worst disasters ever to hit the South Pacific. Its winds raged up to 155 miles per hour, causing widespread devastation on the islands of Vanuatu. Around 75,000 people were left in need of emergency shelter, and 96 percent of food crops were destroyed.

When Cyclone Pam hit the islands of Vanuatu, it destroyed about 80 percent of the buildings there.

53

TORNADOES

Tornadoes are the scariest, wildest windstorms in the world. They may not be the biggest storms, but they have the most powerful winds. A tornado's energy is concentrated in a small area. Its winds spiral tightly down to the ground in a funnel shape, and it destroys anything in its path.

This large tornado is swirling above a green field in Colorado.

Born in a Storm

Tornadoes usually form as part of a thunderstorm. When a mass of cold, dry air meets warm, damp air, the warmer air rises and forms thunderclouds. Sometimes, when the cold air meets the warm air, together they start to spin in a column. Rain and hail then push the spinning air down toward the ground.

Cold air descending (blue arrows)

Rotating wind

Warm air rising (red arrows)

This is how tornadoes form in thunderstorms.

Up in the Air

Tornado winds are so powerful they can lift roofs, vehicles, or sheds off the ground, and fling them around. People have also been carried through the air. In 1955, this happened to a nine-year-old girl who was riding a pony. They both survived.

Tornadoes are smaller and faster than hurricanes, and do not last as long, but they can cause terrible damage.

LIGHTNING FACT

The United Kingdom has more tornadoes than any other place, but the tornadoes are mostly too weak to cause damage.

WATERSPOUTS AND DUST DEVILS

Waterspouts and dust devils are mini-tornadoes that can form over a lake, river, or sea, or over dry, hot, dusty places, such as deserts. They are smaller and weaker than normal tornadoes, and usually not as dangerous. However, waterspouts can still be up to 3,600 feet high and have been known to overturn boats and damage ships on the ocean.

Waterspouts

Waterspouts appear over water but they are not made of solid water—they are mostly made of clouds or mist. A waterspout can grow upward from the water as warm air rises, or it can reach down from a cloud, like a regular tornado.

This waterspout is moving over the ocean.

Dust Devils

A dust devil forms when hot air just above the ground starts to move upward. As it meets the cooler air above it, it begins to twist into a spiral. The moving air sucks up dust or sand, making the dust devil easy to see.

LIGHTNING FACT

In some countries, dust devils were traditionally seen as desert spirits or ghosts.

A waterspout looks like a writhing, watery snake as it stretches between the sea and the clouds.

DUST STORMS AND SANDSTORMS

One of the scariest weather sights is a huge, dark wall of sand or dust rolling toward people. These storms happen when strong winds pick up a lot of desert sand or dusty, dried-out soil. Dust storms and sandstorms can swallow up entire cities, and make it unsafe for aircraft to fly. They are common in dry areas, such as North Africa and Arabia.

Dangerous Dust

A big sandstorm or dust storm can be a horrible experience. The flying particles get in people's eyes and mouths, and down their throats. The storm can make it impossible to see, causing traffic accidents. Sandstorms can also drop huge heaps or drifts of sand that can bury cars, houses, and crops.

A storm blows over a town, covering it in red dust.

58

Haboobs

A haboob is a strong wind that usually happens along the southern edges of the Sahara, and can carry vast amounts of sand or dust. It moves like a thick wall that can reach a height of about 3,300 feet. The term "haboob" is taken from the Arabic word *habb*, meaning "wind."

The city of Dubai in the United Arab Emirates is covered by a sandstorm.

LIGHTNING FACT

Dirt mixed with wind can make dust storms known as black blizzards.

The Dust Bowl

In the United States in the 1930s, a serious drought made a large area of the country horribly dusty and dry. This area became known as the Dust Bowl. Giant dust storms in the area caused people serious illnesses by making it hard for them to breathe.

DUST BOWL

Denver ■

■ Topeka

Santa Fe ■

■ Oklahoma City

Austin

The light area in this map shows the region known as the Dust Bowl

WORLD OF WATER

When people think of weather, they often think of water. Clouds, rain, snow, hail, sleet, mist, and fog are all made of water floating around in the atmosphere. When water comes out of the air and falls to the ground in any form, it is called precipitation. Water constantly moves between the atmosphere and Earth's surface in a process called the **water cycle**.

Water in the Air

The Sun's heat makes water evaporate into the air from oceans, seas, lakes, and rivers. Water also evaporates from damp land and soil. Snow and ice can evaporate directly into gas and float into the air. Plants release water into the air from their leaves.

The water cycle

Water constantly moves around the atmosphere. This is called the water cycle.

How Much Water?

At any one time, the atmosphere contains about 3118.9 cubic miles of water. That is about as much water as there is in a large lake, such as Lake Superior. If all this water fell out of the sky at once, it would cover the world in a layer of water about 1 inch deep.

People in a crowded street in Hong Kong carry colorful umbrellas to keep off the rain.

LIGHTNING FACT

On average, water stays in the air for about nine days before falling to Earth's surface.

Misty Breath

When people and animals breathe out, they breathe water into the air. That is why when they go out on a very cold day, they can see their breaths as "clouds." The cold air makes the water vapor, or gas, from the body condense into droplets that are big enough to see.

When it is very cold, people's breaths make mini-clouds.

CLOUDS

Clouds form when water vapor changes from a gas into tiny water droplets. This happens when the air becomes cooler. In the troposphere—the part of the atmosphere closest to the ground—the air gets cooler the higher up a person goes, so clouds usually form high in the sky. Clouds come in various shapes and types, and each type has its own name. There are three main types of clouds: cumulus, cirrus, and stratus.

LIGHTNING FACT

The classification of clouds is based on a book written in 1803 by Luke Howard, an amateur **meteorologist** in London, England.

Fluffy white clouds like these are cumulus clouds.

Cumulus Clouds

If the water droplets in a cloud are very small and tightly packed, they reflect more light, and the cloud looks white. Cumulus clouds are white and fluffy, with flat bases. They form low in the atmosphere on a sunny day.

Altocumulus

Cumulonimbus

Cirrus

Cirrocumulus

Stratocumulus

Cirrus Clouds

Cirrus clouds are the thin, white, and wispy clouds that look a little like locks of hair. They form high in the atmosphere, usually above heights of about 20,000 feet.

The main types of clouds can combine to form many other types of clouds.

These are altostratus clouds. These clouds bring a storm with continuous rain or snow.

Stratus Clouds

Gray clouds bring rain. This is because the water in the clouds has formed larger droplets that reflect less light, so the cloud looks gray. The undersides of clouds can also look dark because sunlight cannot easily shine through them. Stratus clouds look like gray blankets and bring light, drizzly rain.

STRANGE CLOUDS

Clouds are always changing, and they can take many forms, shapes, and sizes. Once in a while, very odd-looking clouds can form. There are clouds that look like crashing waves, clouds that seem to resemble people or objects, and clouds that have the appearance of **UFOs**. When new cloud shapes are discovered, they are given new names.

Banner clouds rise over the Matterhorn in Switzerland.

Banner Clouds

Banner clouds cling to one side of a mountain. They form as the wind pushes damp air high up a mountainside. They form in a layer and stay in one place for a long time because the wind continuously flows from one direction.

Lenticular Clouds

Lenticular clouds are called "lenticular" because they are shaped like lenses. They usually form over the tops of high mountains as damp air piles up in one place. Some are so round that they look similar to alien spaceships.

At a first glance, this lenticular cloud really looks like a flying saucer.

LIGHTNING FACT

Some UFO sightings may actually have been lenticular clouds.

Mammatus Clouds

A mammatus cloud has strange, sack-like shapes hanging down from its base. Weather scientists are not sure exactly how these shapes form, but they think it has something to do with warm and cool air swirling around in patterns under the cloud.

Mammatus clouds form over Jacksonville in Florida.

WHAT IS RAIN?

Rain is one of the most important types of weather. Thanks to rain, crops and other plants can grow, and people and animals have water to drink. Rain is part of the water cycle, the process by which water circulates between the atmosphere and the planet. Without rain, Earth would be very different.

Medium to heavy raindrops measure about 0.2 inches across. Smaller drops are called drizzle.

Water Droplets

The Sun heats the land and sea, making water evaporate into the air. As the water vapor rises, it cools. In cold air, the water vapor condenses. This means it turns from a gas into a liquid, and forms droplets of water. These water droplets form clouds.

This is the Atacama Desert in Chile. The bone-dry desert receives hardly any rain all year round

Streams, rivers, and waterfalls, such as this one in Thailand, exist only because rain falls on the land.

LIGHTNING FACT

A typical raindrop lands at a speed of about 18.6 miles per hour.

How Rain Forms

As clouds rise higher, they become even colder, and the water in them turns into heavy raindrops. At a certain point, these drops become so big and heavy that the air can no longer hold them up. Gravity pulls them to the ground in the form of rain.

ACID RAIN

Some rain that falls from the sky contains chemicals that are powerful enough to dissolve metal and crumble stone. This acid rain is rain that has been polluted by gases released into the atmosphere by power plants, factories, and gasoline-driven vehicles. Acid rain can wear away the surface of buildings, damage plants and trees, poison lakes, and kill insects and fish.

Winds can carry **pollution** far from where it is released to form acid rain in other places.

How Acid Rain Works

When **fossil fuels** such as coal, natural gas, and oil are burned, they release certain harmful gases into the air. These gases combine with the oxygen and water vapor in the air. When the water in the air condenses and falls to Earth as rain, sleet, hail, or snow, it carries these gases with it.

When sulfur dioxide (SO_2) and nitrogen oxide (NO_2) are released into the air, they can form sulfuric acid (H_2SO_4) and nitrous acid (HNO_2), and make acid rain.

H_2SO_4

Trees killed by acid rain

HNO_2

H_2O

NO_2

SO_2

68

Losing Lake Life

Acid rain can fall directly into lakes and rivers, or wash into these waterways from surrounding land. Acid rain makes the soils in lakes, streams, and wetlands release aluminum. The mix of acidic water and aluminum makes waters **toxic** to crayfish, clams, fish, and other **aquatic** animals.

Reducing Acid Rain

By the early 21st century, many places, including the United States, Canada, and Europe, had introduced controls to reduce the amount of sulfur dioxide released by industries. This has helped many damaged forests recover. However, parts of Asia still have problems.

Acid rain harms the leaves and needles of trees. These damaged trees are in Grayson Highlands State Park in Virginia.

RAINSTORMS

A rainstorm is a period of extra-heavy rain. Rainstorms are more common during hot weather, when more water evaporates from the land and seas. The water droplets in the air then form large rainclouds, which release heavier rain than normal. Heavy rain can damage crops by flattening or swamping them. It can soak into soil on steep slopes and cause landslides or cliff collapses. It can make rivers and lakes overflow.

LIGHTNING FACT

The biggest-ever raindrops were recorded over Brazil and the Pacific Ocean. They were 0.4 inches across.

A deep, low cloud such as this can release a sudden rainstorm.

Sudden Downpour

In a heavy rainstorm, raindrops are big and close together. A lot of water falls in a short space of time. If the rain falls onto soil or plants on fairly flat land, it can soak into the ground. When heavy rain falls in hilly areas, it can end up rushing down into valleys or lower areas, causing floods.

How Wet Does It Get?

The wettest parts of the world are mainly in the tropics. This is where the weather is warmest, and where most water evaporates into the atmosphere. Some of the wettest places include Hawaii, West Africa, northern India, and Colombia.

Heavy rain soaking into soil can cause dangerous landslides, such as this one in Japan.

Wettest Place to Live

Several places claim to be the wettest in the world, but most experts agree that the village of Mawsynram in India holds the record. This village has an average rainfall of 467 inches a year—enough rain to cover a four-story building!

Floods like this one in Bangkok, Thailand, can disrupt railroad lines and roads and make travel difficult.

4212   4212

FLOODS AND FLASH FLOODS

In a flood, water flows over land that is normally dry. Some rivers flood every year, watering the fields around them, but if a flood happens where people live, it can be devastating. If people know a flood is coming, they usually head for higher ground. Some people move their possessions upstairs first, and surround their homes with sandbags to try to keep out water.

LIGHTNING FACT

Floods have caused some of the worst natural disasters in history.

When the local river flooded, it flowed through the streets of Steyr, Austria.

Flood Damage

Fast-flowing floodwater can trap or sweep away houses and cars. Floods can cut off electricity and clean-water supplies. Floodwater can be dirty and smelly, and it can spread diseases. When a flood dries up, it leaves damp, muddy **silt** everywhere.

72

Flood Causes

During heavy rains, soil can become saturated to the point where no more rain can soak into it. Then, the rainwater flows off the soil and into rivers instead. When rivers fill up, they overflow their banks and cause floods. Sea storms and rising sea levels can also cause floods (see pages 76–77).

A view from the air shows cars and trucks on a flooded road in Colombia, South America.

The steep slopes of the Alps led to this flash flood in Chamonix, France.

Flash Floods

Flash floods are very sudden, surprise floods. They usually happen when heavy rain quickly flows down mountainsides or hills into valleys. A flash flood can affect an area far away from where it is actually raining, making it even more unexpected.

73

FLOOD CASE STUDIES

Storms, typhoons, and other extreme weather can cause floods. Floods can happen almost anywhere in the world but these are some of the most recent.

Carolina, United States 2015

After heavy rain in the region of Carolina, floods caused chaos. In total, 17 people died either by drowning or as a result of traffic accidents caused by the weather. Hundreds of roads had to be closed and some were completely washed away.

Kuttanad in India is an area below sea level and is often affected by floods during heavy rains, such as those in 2013.

India 2013

In June 2013, rain lasting several days caused devastating floods and landslides in northern India. Nearly 6,000 people died, roads and bridges were destroyed, and more than 110,000 people were **evacuated**.

United Kingdom 2015

December 2015 was the wettest month in the United Kingdom since records began in 1910. Almost double the average rain fell. Rivers burst their banks, causing widespread flooding that disrupted roads, communications, and power supplies. Farms and more than 16,000 homes were flooded.

The storm that hit Carolina in 2015 washed away entire sections of highway.

The army used boats to rescue people from flooded homes in York city center in the United Kingdom in December 2015.

Malawi 2015

In 2015, terrible floods devastated Malawi in Africa, affecting nearly 250,000 people. Around 230,000 people were forced to flee their homes. Hundreds of people were injured or killed, fields of crops were ruined, livestock killed, and homes swept away.

These people in Malawi are carrying their crops as they cross a flooded road during 2015 floods.

SEA FLOODS

Many people would love to live in a house by the coast, but what happens when seawater crashes onto the land and floods towns along the shore? In the past, storm surges were the main cause of flooding by the sea. However, as the sea level generally rises all across the world as a result of global warming (see pages 124–125), sea floods may occur more often with **high tides**.

This storm along the coastline in Beirut, Lebanon, could cause seawater to surge onto land.

LIGHTNING FACT

Most of the people who died when Hurricane Katrina hit the Gulf Coast of the United States in 2005 were killed by the storm surge it caused.

Storm Surge

High winds and low air pressure forming over the sea cause storm surges. High winds push the seawater toward the coast, and low pressure causes the sea to rise higher than normal because it does not have as much air pushing down on it. This can cause extensive flooding.

Seawater flooded Samutprakarna, Thailand, during floods in 2009.

Rising Water

Normally, a slight rise in sea level is not a problem. However, if there are also strong winds, a high tide, and low-lying land, it can be disastrous. Hurricanes often create storm surges. When the extra-high seawater reaches the coast, the water, pushed by the strong winds, rushes ashore.

A storm surge caused by Hurricane Sandy in New Jersey, 2012, damaged cars and property.

Deadly Surge

In 1970, one of the deadliest storm surges in history struck Bangladesh and India after a cyclone formed in the Indian Ocean. Many of the flat islands and coastal areas there were swamped and 500,000 people died.

This map shows the location of the 1970 storm surge that hit Bangladesh and India.

India

Bangladesh

Indian Ocean

FOG AND MIST

Although clouds are normally found high in the sky, they can also form close to the ground. When this happens, the cloud is called fog or mist. Just like a cloud, fog and mist are made of water droplets floating in the air. The droplets form when damp air becomes very cold, and the water vapor in the air condenses into tiny drops of liquid, which are light enough to float instead of falling as rain.

San Francisco, California, is famous for its coastal fogs.

Drivers should travel more slowly in fog to be safe. In thick fog, they should avoid driving altogether.

Fog or Mist?

Fog and mist are the same thing, but fog is thicker. Mist is thinner because it contains fewer water droplets than fog. If people can see for at least 0.6 miles, they are in mist. If the **visibility** is worse and they cannot see that far, they are in fog.

Where Does Fog Form?

Fog happens close to the ground on a winter morning, after the very cold ground has cooled the air. It occurs in valleys, where cold air sinks and collects at the bottom. Fog appears at sea, when the wind blows damp air over cold seawater.

Morning mists can create shadowy scenes like this one in a valley in Taipei, Taiwan.

LIGHTNING FACT

Very thick fog, with visibility below 328 feet, can cause traffic accidents.

Mist often forms when the warmer air over a lake meets the cooler surface of land.

HAZE AND SMOG

Haze looks a little like a mist but, instead of water droplets, haze is made up of tiny particles of dust, smoke, or salt. Weather conditions such as humidity and lack of wind mean the pollution hangs around, rather than being dispersed. The particles in haze are barely visible individually, but together, they cause a reduction in visibility.

In big Chinese cities such as Shenyang, many people wear masks to prevent breathing in haze or smog particles.

LIGHTNING FACT

In 2013, air pollution led to more than 5.5 million people dying earlier than they should have.

Killer Smog

Smog is a mixture of pollution and fog. It often forms in cities because water droplets condense easily around tiny specks of dust or smoke in the air. It can cause breathing problems and make people sick. By reducing visibility, smog can cause traffic accidents.

Polluted Air

Most of the particles in the air that cause haze and smog are released when fossil fuels, such as gasoline and coal, are burned in power stations, vehicles, or factories. Some haze and smog conditions occur when there are widespread forest fires.

In slow-moving traffic, vehicles release a lot of fumes that contribute to smog.

Smoke from forest fires burning in Indonesia has caused this haze across Singapore.

RAINBOWS

There are few weather sights more beautiful than a rainbow arching across the sky. Long ago, people thought rainbows were magical because they are so perfectly shaped and they shine with bright colors. To occur, rainbows need two things—sunlight and raindrops. To see a rainbow, people must have the Sun behind them and the raindrops in front of them.

People see a whole rainbow because they are looking at many raindrops, all bending and separating the Sun's light.

What Makes a Rainbow?

Sunlight is "white" light, which is made up of many colors. When a ray of white light shines into a raindrop, the ray bends and reflects off the back of the raindrop, and the colors separate and spread out to form a rainbow.

LIGHTNING FACT

There are usually seven colors in a rainbow: red, orange, yellow, green, blue, indigo, and violet.

A rainbow called a "moonbow" happens when the light reflected off the surface of the Moon refracts off the droplets of water in the atmosphere.

Rainbows Everywhere

Rainbows are not only seen in rain. They are also noticeable in fog, misty clouds, or the spray from a waterfall. People can even make their own rainbows by standing with their backs to the Sun and spraying a fine mist with a hose.

Sometimes, a double rainbow can be seen. This happens when light reflects twice inside the water droplets of rain.

WIND AND WAVES

Boats make waves as they push through water, and people make waves when they jump into the sea. However, the wind makes most of the waves that are seen on an ocean. The height of waves depends on the speed of the wind, how long the wind blows for, and how far it blows in the same direction.

Huge waves break over the lighthouse and pier in Douro harbor, Portugal.

Where Do Waves Come From?

Out at sea, wind blows over the surface of the water, pushing and disturbing it so that it ripples and forms waves. The stronger the wind, and the longer it blows, the bigger the waves will be. Waves also grow bigger when the wind blows them over a long distance.

Why Waves Break

At sea, waves ripple forward through the water, but rarely break. As they approach the shore, they move into shallower water. As the bottom part of the wave drags over the seabed, the top part piles up, tips over, and breaks.

A surfer rides along the steep front of a huge wave as it rolls forward and breaks.

Dangerous Waves

In a storm, especially when there is a storm surge (see pages 76–77), big waves can pour over sea walls and smash up railroads, roads, and buildings. They may even wash away people who are too close.

The **friction** between the wind and the water causes waves on the water's surface.

SEICHES

A seiche is a rare event. It is the sloshing back and forth of water in a lake or an enclosed bay. It is like water in a bathtub when someone stirs it. Lake water sloshes to and fro all the time, but usually the change in water level is not noticeable. A severe seiche can cause water to flood onto the shore and put lives at risk.

Wind causes a local rise in water level called wind setup.

Wind direction

High water due to wind setup

Still water level

Sloshing Water

With a seiche, strong storm winds, high air pressure, or movements from a volcano, earthquake, or landslide can make the water move so that it sinks in one area and rises in another. The water then sloshes back the opposite way.

Seiches can cause the water in an enclosed body of water to push to and fro for hours or even days.

High waves flow over the pier in Lake Michigan.

A combination of seiches, wind, and high tides caused this flood in Venice, Italy.

Seiche Disaster

A deadly seiche struck Lake Michigan in 1954. As the water level rose near the city of Chicago, Illinois, it reached a height of more than 9.8 feet. It caused damage along the shore and washed away people who were fishing on a pier. Eight of them drowned.

87

EL NIÑO

El Niño is a warm ocean current in the Pacific Ocean that can cause extreme weather events across the world. El Niño events happen roughly every two to seven years, when the ocean current shifts position around the equator, making some places wetter, and others much hotter, than usual. These changes can cause droughts, floods, disease, and billions of dollars of damage.

In 2007, severe flooding caused by an El Niño event destroyed these houses in Jakarta, Indonesia.

How El Niño Happens

In most years, the trade winds blow across the Pacific from east to west. They push warm surface water toward Australia and Indonesia. During an El Niño, the trade winds are weak or blow in the opposite direction, so warm surface water piles up near the west coast of South America.

El Niño Effects

The flow of warm water to the eastern Pacific can cause storms on the Pacific coast, bringing heavy rains and flooding. El Niño has the opposite effect on the western side of the Pacific. There, droughts, heat waves, and wildfires occur because so little rain falls.

In Australia, El Niño causes lower than average rainfall and warmer temperatures, and worsens droughts.

What Is La Niña?

La Niña, meaning "the little girl," is the opposite to El Niño ("the little boy"). During a La Niña year, waters of the tropical eastern Pacific are colder than normal, and trade winds blow more strongly than usual. This makes it warmer in the southeast and cooler than normal in the northwest.

La Niña rains caused massive flooding in the city and airport in Bangkok, Thailand, in 2011

SNOWSTORMS AND BLIZZARDS

When there is a storm and snow together, the weather can be very extreme. In a snowstorm, a lot of snow falls and builds up on the ground. If strong winds blow the snow in all directions as it falls, the snowstorm is called a blizzard, or "whiteout." It can be almost impossible for people to see where they are going during a blizzard.

Severe snowstorms often cause traffic jams and delays. These drivers have come to a standstill.

People on snowmobiles enjoy the snow in New York state, after snowstorms hit the area in 2009.

Lost in the Snow

In a severe blizzard, the whiteout can be so bad that people cannot see in front of their faces. People have been known to become lost in blizzards even when they were very close to houses and safety.

Watch Out for Windchill

Wind can make the temperature feel much colder than it actually is. This is called the "windchill factor." Just as a breeze can cool people on a hot day, when it is cold, wind can make them feel even colder.

Snowplows clear snow from main roads after a blizzard.

LIGHTNING FACT

In 1911, in Tamarack, Idaho, 36 feet of snow fell in one month.

Snow Dangers

Heavy snow is fun for sledding, snowballing, and building snowmen, but it causes many problems. Deep snow makes it hard for vehicles to operate. Large snowdrifts can trap people inside houses. The weight of snow can make gutters and roofs collapse, and bring down tree branches.

93

AVALANCHES

An avalanche happens when a mass of snow piles up on a slope and becomes so heavy that it suddenly slips downhill. Avalanches can be small, but in high mountain ranges, such as the Alps in Europe and the Himalayas in Asia, they are often huge and very dangerous.

LIGHTNING FACT

Each year, avalanches kill more than 150 people worldwide.

A huge avalanche rushes down a high mountain in the Caucasus region of Russia.

Buried by Snow

Avalanches are a risk for skiers and mountain hikers. The heavy, fast-moving snow can crush and injure anyone it lands on. The snow can also bury people so that they cannot breathe. Some avalanches have buried entire villages and even towns.

Surviving an Avalanche

In an avalanche, people should drop heavy bags, because these will make them sink, and run sideways. They should try to "swim" with their arms to stay on top of the moving snow. If people become buried, they should hold their hands in front of their faces and dig a hole in the snow to help themselves breathe.

Barriers like these can stop avalanches from flowing all the way down a slope and burying towns or villages below.

Skiers wear packs with airbags that inflate in the event of an avalanche. The packs keep the skiers above the sliding mass of snow.

95

HAIL

When it starts to hail, people usually run for cover because rock-solid balls of ice can really hurt, even when they are normal, pea-sized hailstones. Hailstones can be much bigger and they can cause serious damage. They can dent vehicles and smash windows, damage roofs, flatten crops, and cut off power supplies.

Caught in a sudden hailstorm, these people are running to safety.

How Hail Happens

Hail forms in tall thunderclouds with fast-moving air currents. When water droplets blow to the top of the cloud, where it is freezing cold, they turn into balls of ice. As they are blown around in the cloud, more layers of ice build up on them. When they become too heavy, they fall as hail.

Hailstones are normally the size of peas but they can be much bigger.

Hail Swaths

Hailstorms are usually sudden and heavy, and last for just a few minutes. During this time, they often move across the land, leaving a long, narrow trail of hail. This is called a hail swath, and it leaves piles of hailstones on the ground in its wake.

A ten-minute hailstorm in Buenos Aires, Argentina, in 2013, left 5,000 cars damaged by hailstones that were the size of golf balls!

If a large hailstone is cut in half, its layers of ice can be seen. These layers are similar to the growth rings in a slice of a tree's trunk.

Record Hailstones

The biggest hailstones are made up of a lot of smaller hailstones clumped together. The largest recorded hailstone fell in South Dakota in 2010. At 7.8 inches across, it was as big as a melon!

FROST AND DEW

Frost and dew can be seen in the morning after a cool, clear night. Dew is water that condenses from the air onto outdoor surfaces when the temperature drops overnight. It forms droplets of water on plants near the ground. In very cold weather, dew forms as ice, and it is called frost. The ice crystals in frost can form delicate shapes that make frost appear spiky, fluffy, or furry.

Window Frost

In freezing weather, frost can form on the inside of an ice-cold window. When moisture in the air touches the window, it freezes into ice crystals. As the crystals spread, they can form patterns that look like feathers, trees, or ferns.

Frost can create a pretty coating on fruits, twigs, and leaves.

Hoar frost is white, flaky frost that forms overnight on cold objects.

Droplets of morning dew reveal the beautiful shapes that make up a spider's web.

Frost Damage

Frost can form a coat of ice over plants and freeze the water inside them. This can damage some plants, which may turn black and die. Farmers have seen entire fields of their crops destroyed by just a few frosty nights.

LIGHTNING FACT

Hoar frost gets its name from a word meaning "old," because it looks like white hair.

HOW COLD DOES IT GET?

Water freezes at 32 degrees Fahrenheit, so when the temperature drops this low, snow or ice may fall, and it feels cold outside. However, it can get a lot colder than 32 degrees Fahrenheit. Antarctica, the landmass around the South Pole, is the world's coldest place. At the South Pole, the average temperature is about -56 degrees Fahrenheit, which is much colder than a kitchen freezer.

Snow, ice, and huge glaciers, such as this one, still cover most of Greenland.

Ice Ages

There have been several ice ages. An ice age is a long period of time when it is much colder than it is now. About 20,000 years ago, it was so cold that glaciers covered the land around the North Pole, reaching as far south as today's London, in England, and to New York City.

In very low temperatures, people wear hats and scarves over their face to keep their nose, fingers, and toes from freezing.

Antarctica is the world's most southern-most point and its climate is the coldest on Earth.

Coldest Weather Ever

The coldest weather recorded was -128.56 degrees Fahrenheit, measured at Vostok research station in Antarctica, in 1983. That is almost as far below zero as boiling is above zero. It can be colder than this high up in Earth's atmosphere, but weather temperatures are always recorded at ground level.

LIGHTNING FACT

In 1684, it was so cold that the River Thames in London, England, remained frozen for two months.

WEIRD WEATHER

Most weather—even something as striking as a rainbow—is quite familiar. However, once in a while, weather can be very weird. It can put on an amazing display of lights, shower people with animals, or make people see things that are not there!

Sun halos look about eight times as wide as the Sun.

The aurora borealis or Northern Lights, seen in northern Canada.

Amazing Auroras

Auroras are moving patterns of light that sometimes appear in the sky. They happen when particles from the Sun meet Earth's upper atmosphere. Auroras near the North Pole are called *aurora borealis*, and those near the South Pole are known as *aurora australis*.

Mirages often occur in deserts or on hot road surfaces. This is a mirage in the Sahara, Africa.

Halos

A halo is a huge ring of light around the Sun, or sometimes the Moon. Halos are caused by bright sunlight or moonlight shining through crystals of ice in the atmosphere. As well as a halo, sometimes you see two bright spots of light on either side of the Sun. These are known as "sun dogs."

Making Mirages

Mirages happen when layers of air are at different temperatures. As light passes between layers, it bends. When light beams from a blue sky pass through cool air into warm air, they bend upward. This means blue light appears to be coming from the ground, and the brain is tricked into thinking it is water.

UNUSUAL RAIN

Sometimes, when it is raining heavily, people say that it is "raining cats and dogs." Although it never actually rains cats and dogs, fish and frogs can fall from the sky like rain. There have also been rare cases of bright red rain—so red that it looks like blood—falling from the sky.

LIGHTNING FACT

Some people have reported seeing snakes, worms, and spiders falling as rain.

Fish and Frogs

Animal rain is rare but, occasionally, it does happen. Experts think that, sometimes, a waterspout sucks up a shoal of fish from the sea, or a tornado sucks up frogs or tadpoles from a pond. Soon afterward, the animals fall back down in a shower.

If you were to see fish raining from the skies, it might look a little like this!

Red Dust

Winds whipping up reddish dust from desert areas cause red rain. The dust is carried into rainclouds, where the raindrops condense around the dust particles. If there is a lot of dust, the rain looks red as it falls, and leaves red stains behind when it dries up.

Algae, a type of living organism, are sometimes bright red, as shown here. They can become mixed with water and fall as red rain.

Red Rain

In 2001, red rain fell in Kerala, in southern India. Under a microscope, the rain was found to contain tiny, reddish cells. Some experts suggested the cells could have come from space, but others said they were from local algae found growing on trees, rocks, and lampposts.

Cells from Kerala's red rain as seen through a microscope.

STRANGE LIGHTNING

Large flashes of volcanic lightning sometimes happen in the cloud of ash above an erupting volcano. Experts think that particles of air, ash, and dust moving around in the cloud build up an electrical charge, as in a thundercloud.

You can clearly see a brilliant flash of volcanic lightning during this eruption in Iceland.

In 1753, a scientist named Georg Richmann was in the process of carrying out an experiment when ball lightning struck him on the head. It killed him instantly.

Balls of Fire

Ball lightning appears as a glowing ball of fire that floats through the air during a thunderstorm. The lightning burns everything that it touches. While normal lightning happens thousands of times a day around the world, ball lightning is so rare that most people never see it.

St. Elmo's Fire

St. Elmo's fire is a blue or purple glow that sometimes appears around objects during a storm. This phenomena happens when electrical energy creates a charge that sparks out from a sharp or pointed object, such as a church tower or an airplane's tail.

St. Elmo's fire is seen here on the cockpit window of an aircraft.

Jets and Sprites

Jets and sprites are bursts of colored lightning that happen high in the atmosphere, above thunderstorms. They were discovered in the late 20th century by high-flying aircraft pilots. Red sprites look like huge jellyfish, while blue jets are narrow and shoot up from the tops of storms.

LIGHTNING FACT

Ball lightning can pass right through walls and windows.

The red patch here is a sprite above the United States.

UNDERSTANDING THE WEATHER

The science of weather is called meteorology, and weather scientists are known as meteorologists. Meteorologists do not just study how weather works, they also forecast the weather, predicting what will happen based on the way weather patterns are moving. Accurate forecasts help many people—for example, they tell farmers when it is dry enough to harvest their crops and fishermen when it is too stormy to go to sea.

LIGHTNING FACT

The first weather satellite to send back pictures to Earth was launched in 1960.

Weather Forecasts

Weather forecasts are made by inputting measurements and other **data** into computers that turn the information into weather maps. Using special software, forecasters can calculate how the weather patterns will change over the next few days, and where it will be windy, rainy, sunny, or snowy.

A weather forecaster prepares a weather report using data from many different sources.

Measuring the Weather

Meteorologists use many different measuring instruments. As well as taking measurements themselves, they collect data from **weather buoys** at sea, **weather balloons** in the sky, and automatic weather stations. Weather satellites above Earth also take measurements and photographs of weather systems.

Weather balloons are launched into the sky to collect weather data from the atmosphere.

Meteorologists collect data about the weather at stations, such as this one in the Carpathian Mountains, Ukraine.

MEASURING WEATHER

Meteorologists measure the weather all over the world. To ensure that they can compare the weather in their area to the rest of the world, meteorologists use standard equipment so that they get standard measurements. For example, they use similar thermometers to measure temperature, sunshine recorders to measure the brightness of the sun, and hail pads made of foam that reveal the size of the hailstones that fall into them.

The Saffir-Simpson scale is a one-to-five rating based on a hurricane's wind speed. This is Hurricane Patricia, a scale-five hurricane.

Measuring Wind

Wind direction is reported by the direction from where the wind blows. For example, although wind blowing from the west is traveling eastward, it is called a westerly wind, not an easterly wind. Wind speed is measured using an anemometer, and air pressure is measured with a barometer.

Thermometers usually measure temperature in degrees Fahrenheit and Celsius.

Measuring Rain

Weather scientists record rainfall using an instrument called a rain gauge. This measures the amount of rain that falls over a certain period of time. Rain falls into the top of the gauge and collects at the bottom, where it can be measured against a scale bar.

This is a mobile weather station. It has equipment to measure different kinds of weather, including humidity, wind speed, and temperature.

Weather Scales

Meteorologists use specially designed weather scales for some extreme types of weather:
- The Beaufort scale measures wind speed and damage.
- The Saffir-Simpson scale measures hurricane intensity.
- The Torro scale measures hailstorm intensity and size.
- The Fujita scale measures tornado strength and severity.

WEATHER MAPS

In a televised weather forecast, the forecaster usually stands next to a map and may show different types of maps featuring the same place to explain different aspects of the weather. In early televised weather forecasts, forecasters would put cloud, rain, or sunshine stickers onto a wall map. Modern television weather maps are computer-generated, and often animated, but they still use simple symbols for different types of weather.

LIGHTNING FACT

People have been forecasting the weather for at least 3,000 years.

Symbols such as these make it easy for people to understand weather forecasts at a glance.

More on Maps

As well as using symbols to indicate rain, sunshine, and clouds, weather maps use different colors to show temperature—green and blue for colder areas, and orange and red for warmer weather. The predicted temperatures can also appear in degrees.

Map Lines

Lines on weather maps are called isobars. Isobars join points that have the same atmospheric pressure. They show areas of low and high pressure. Winds blow from high to low pressure, so isobars on a map tell people about wind strength and direction.

Forecasters use isobars to show how high- and low-pressure air masses are moving across an area.

STORM TRACKING

Most people find it useful to know what the weather will be in the coming days—especially if an enormous storm is forecast. When a tropical cyclone, such as a typhoon, is detected over an ocean, forecasters use data from satellites and weather stations to track it and to predict its path. This enables them to calculate when and where it will hit land and how strong it will be.

Storm Warning

Storm tracking allows warnings to be **broadcast** to tell people a storm is on its way. This gives people time to board up their houses, evacuate the area, or get to a storm shelter. When Typhoon Hagupit made landfall in the Philippines on December 6, 2014, the advance warnings saved many lives.

People in the Philippines rush to an evacuation center to escape the strong winds and heavy rain of Typhoon Hagupit.

The Cyclone's Path

As a tropical cyclone moves across the ocean, it can travel in a straight line or a gentle curve. Sometimes, cyclones can also change direction. Their path depends on the following things: the location, size, and speed of the storm; other winds in the area; areas of high or low pressure in the area; and the way Earth spins.

This tornado is racing across fields in South Colorado.

People need tornado warnings such as this siren to help them get to safety.

Storm Chasers

Storm chasers are people who follow tornadoes to take photographs or to film storms. They follow tornadoes by car, or sometimes by airplane or helicopter. Storm chasers often report their tornado sightings to weather forecasters to help them predict where the tornado will go next.

WEATHER SATELLITES

Satellites are objects that orbit Earth. Humans have sent many types of satellites into orbit. Some are used to study the stars, some carry Internet signals, and others monitor Earth's weather by watching it from above. They send images and information to computers on Earth. Space shuttles and rockets carry satellites into space.

Weather Monitor

Weather satellites usually make images of Earth that can reveal weather patterns. They have cameras that sense the same kind of light that people can see, and infrared sensors to detect heat. Some use extremely sensitive light sensors to find lightning, forest fires, and volcanic eruptions.

This Meteosat weather satellite image shows the weather systems over Europe and Africa.

Satellites at Work

The solar panels on the outside of a weather satellite provide electricity to power the cameras and other weather instruments that the satellite carries. Satellites also have sunshades to shield the detecting telescopes and cameras. A transmitter is used to send data to receivers on Earth.

Meteosat is a weather satellite. Its instruments scan Earth for tropical storms and other weather events.

This weather satellite image shows snow and snow clouds covering Ireland.

Still or Moving?

Weather satellites in **geostationary** orbits always hover at around 22,370 miles above the equator. Other satellites circle over the Poles. They can travel as close as 500 miles to the surface, and take detailed pictures of weather patterns all over the world.

WEATHER LORE

Before modern weather forecasting instruments were invented, people used the colors and patterns of clouds, or how animals and plants behaved, to predict the weather. For example, some types of pine cones close up when there is water in the air, and open when it is dry—so pine cones can help predict rainy weather.

Cows and Rain

People sometimes say that when cows lie down, rain is on the way. Scientists think that cows stand up in hot weather to cool their undersides, and lie down when it is colder. Cold weather often brings rain, so the saying could be true.

When cows lie down, it might be wise to carry an umbrella.

A ring around the Moon is caused by ice crystals in the air. Ice crystals can sink lower and form rain clouds, so there is some truth in the saying "A ring around the Moon means rain upon you soon."

This spectacular sunset has turned the whole sky red, which could mean good weather is due.

Red Skies

"Red sky at night, shepherd's delight. Red sky in the morning, shepherd's warning," is a well-known saying. Reddish sunsets and sunrises are caused by dust particles in dry, warm air. A red sunset means dusty air is in the west and moving toward you, bringing fine weather. A red sunrise means the good weather is in the east, and so it has passed by.

LIGHTNING FACT

Animals sometimes behave strangely when a thunderstorm is on the way—for example, dogs might bark when a storm is approaching.

CLIMATE CHANGE

The climate has changed several times over Earth's history, since the planet formed more than 4.5 billion years ago. In the distant past, it warmed up and cooled down over long periods. These changes took place over millions of years and they were mainly a result of natural causes.

Imagine living at a time when most of Europe and North America were covered in ice like this.

Changing Continents

One reason climates in different places changed was that the continents have changed position. Today, there are seven continents but, in the past, there were only one or two landmasses. Some places with cold climates moved to places with warmer climates and vice versa.

Long ago the hot, dry Sahara in Africa had a cool, wet climate and the land had rivers flowing through it.

Why Climate Change Happens

In the past, events such as volcanic eruptions caused some temporary periods of climate change. The dust from volcanoes blocked out the sunlight, reducing the amount of heat reaching Earth's surface, making it cooler.

Scientists think volcanic eruptions were responsible for a mini ice age in Europe in the Middle Ages.

LIGHTNING FACT

The last ice age ended about 11,000 years ago.

GLOBAL WARMING

Over the last century, scientists have found that Earth is heating up unusually fast—a condition known as global warming. World temperatures have risen more quickly in the past 140 years than at any other time in the past 1,400 years. The other difference with today's climate change is that scientists believe that humans are causing the changes, not nature.

LIGHTNING FACT

Average temperatures today are 33.4 degrees Fahrenheit higher than they were in 1880.

Causes of Global Warming

Scientists think that pollution causes global warming. When people burn fossil fuels, such as coal, oil, and natural gas, they add "greenhouse gases," including **carbon dioxide**, to the air. These gases help trap heat in Earth's atmosphere, increasing the greenhouse effect.

Scientists use satellite images of the poles to help them figure out how fast polar ice caps are melting.

A scientist uses complex equipment to study global warming at the North Pole.

Studying Climate Changes

Scientists look at records of temperatures and study satellite images from the past to see how Earth's temperature is changing today. They also take samples of ice from below the poles that contain bubbles of air. The gases inside reveal what the climate was like thousands of years ago.

The burning gases coming from this chimney are adding greenhouse gases to the atmosphere.

125

A WARMER PLANET

Global warming affects the planet in several ways. The world is getting warmer, there are more cases of extreme weather, and ice caps and glaciers are melting. These changes have a huge impact on humans, plants, and animals. The governments of many countries are coming together to try to reduce greenhouse gas emissions and slow down global warming.

Getting Wetter

Hotter temperatures mean more water evaporating into the air—and so more rain. That means there will be more floods. Ice at the poles is melting into the sea, causing sea levels to rise. Rising sea levels makes it easier for storm surges, big waves, and high tides to flow over the tops of sea walls and onto the land.

A huge chunk of ice breaks off a glacier in Argentina.

LIGHTNING FACT

In the last 100 years, sea levels have risen by 7.8 inches and they are still rising.

Hotter and Wilder

When hot places become hotter, the chances of drought and wildfires are increased. Warmer temperatures in cooler places allow disease-causing insects to go farther north. More places are experiencing extreme weather events such as more lightning and much stronger hurricanes.

There may be more severe heat waves in the future as a result of global warming.

Threats to Wildlife

Certain animals may be killed off because of global warming. For example, polar bears hunt from floating rafts of ice, and as these melt, the bears starve. As ocean temperatures rise, the animals that build coral reefs may die and the animals that live and breed in the reefs will be at risk.

Warmer water can kill beautiful coral reefs that are home to many animals.

127

ENERGY FROM WEATHER

The fossil fuels that humans burn for heating, to power vehicles, and to generate electricity, make the waste gases that are thought to contribute to global warming. The other problem with fossil fuels is that, one day, they will run out, so people are developing ways of collecting energy from other sources, including the weather. Energy can be produced from different types of weather, such as wind and sunshine.

Renewable Energy

Energy sources such as the Sun, wind, and moving water will never run out, so they are called **renewable energy** sources. Producing energy from the weather creates less pollution and less global warming than energy from fossil fuels.

Solar Power

Some solar power stations use the Sun's heat to boil water and create steam. This steam is then used to turn a **turbine** and power a **generator** to make electricity. Some solar energy is created using **photovoltaic cells**, which are often used to power small, portable devices.

Solar panels can be used to power traffic signals.

Hydroelectric power stations use energy from water flowing downhill

The power of the wind turns the blades of a wind turbine. A generator converts the turning force into a flow of electricity.

Wind Power

Wind turbines have blades at the top of tall towers that turn with the wind. They are used along with generators to convert the movement energy from the rotating blades into electricity. Large groups of turbines erected in windy places on Earth are called wind farms.

129

WATER AND EROSION

Weather not only affects people's daily lives, health, and safety, but it also transforms Earth. Wind, heat, cold, rain, and moving water can wear away the surface of rocks. This is called weathering. When those forms of weather also carry away the broken rocks, this is called erosion. Weathering and erosion can create deep valleys, eat away at coastlines, and wear away mountains.

Water Erosion

Heavy rains can make rivers flow faster and stronger. This helps them carry away more rocks and soil along the river bed, carving out deeper channels. When a river dries up, the gash it leaves in the land is called a gorge or valley.

During very heavy rainstorms, water can wash topsoil into rivers and streams.

The Cheddar River cut a gorge that is 400 feet deep and 3 miles long. It is the biggest gorge in the United Kingdom.

Rain Erosion

The impact of heavy raindrops repeatedly hitting an area of soil can loosen particles of earth from the surface. During long storms, the rain can wash the top layer of soil a long distance away. This ruins the land because plants grow best in the fertile top layer of soil, called topsoil.

Large waves can erode and damage coastlines.

Wave Power

When storm winds whip up strong waves, the waves pound against the rocks on the shore. They can split apart tiny cracks so that bigger pieces of rock fall into the sea and are washed away. The waves create bays and **headlands** and can destroy or shift whole beaches of sand.

LIGHTNING FACT

Coastal erosion is worse when extreme weather, such as hurricanes, hits the shore.

WIND AND ICE EROSION

Most people have experienced the power of a strong wind as it blasts against their bodies or the way ice can coat every surface and make things feel brittle. Wind and ice are also capable of breaking up rocks and altering the landscape.

Wind Erosion

Strong winds can carry sand for miles in a sandstorm. When wind blows grains of sand up hard against an area of rock, the sand slowly wears away the surface layer of the rock. The wind and sand can create incredible shapes as they carve away large areas of rock.

Erosion caused the rock formations at Bryce Canyon National Park in Utah.

A glacier created this U-shaped valley in the Alps in Europe.

Glaciers move slowly down slopes as a result of the force of gravity.

Ice Erosion

Glaciers are giant, slow-moving rivers of ice. As a glacier moves, the rocks in its base slowly wear away, or erode, the land below. They leave behind a U-shaped valley. A U-shaped valley is a sign that an area was once covered in ice and home to a giant glacier.

133

POWER OF THE WEATHER

The weather is a powerful thing. It affects people's lives on a daily basis, for example, by dictating what they choose to wear and disrupting outdoor events. Extreme weather has more serious implications, such as tourist industries being ruined when a hurricane destroys a coastal resort or people dying from a heat wave. If global warming results in more severe weather, the weather could have an even greater impact on people's lives in the future.

The effects of global warming are likely to bring more extreme weather events.

How People Adapt

Humans have been adapting to the weather throughout history. During hot Mediterranean summers, people sometimes take afternoon naps called a siesta to avoid the worst of the heat. In Vietnam, people build their homes on stilts to protect them from the monsoon rains.

In some places, people build their houses on stilts to protect them from flooding if sea levels rise.

Rafts of crops floating on a lake in Myanmar.

LIGHTNING FACT

Some farmers in Bangladesh are making floating farms—rafts that grow crops on flood water.

Forward Thinking

In the future, people may need more adaptations. People are already building more defenses to protect coastal settlements from a rise in sea level. In places that are getting hotter and drier, people are looking at ways to reduce the amount of water they use, and farmers may need to plant different crops to cope with changing weather.

135

WEATHER RECORDS

The weather is always setting records. These are some extreme examples from the United States.

MOST EXTREME TORNADO

The Tri-State Tornado hit Missouri, Illinois, and Indiana on March 18, 1925. It set these tornado records:
- Longest path length at 219 miles
- Longest lasting at 3.5 hours
- Fastest forward speed at 73 miles per hour

Heat waves cause devastating damage to farmers' crops.

DEADLIEST HEAT WAVE

The heat waves of summer 1988 caused between 5,000 and 10,000 deaths, ranking them among the world's deadliest. The drought that accompanied the heat waves affected nearly half the United States and led to terrible wildfires and crop failures.

FASTEST WIND

In Oklahoma on May 3, 1999, the wind in a tornado reached a speed of 318 miles per hour.

Tornadoes in the United States can cause damage that costs billions of dollars.

SUNNIEST PLACE

The town of Yuma, in Arizona, gets about 4,020 hours of sunshine per year, making it the sunniest inhabited spot in the United States.

This is an aerial view of Yuma in Arizona, which is on record as being one of the sunniest places in the world.

GREAT WEATHER PIONEERS

People have always been fascinated by the weather. These are some of the most famous meteorologists in the world, who have helped us understand just how weather works.

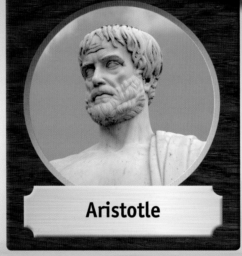

Aristotle

Aristotle (384–322 BCE)
Ancient Greek scientist Aristotle was one of the first people to study the weather in detail. In his book *Meteorology*, he described several types of weather and explained how the water cycle works.

Pliny the Elder

Pliny the Elder (23–79 CE)
The Roman naturalist Pliny wrote a work called *Natural History*, which included detailed explanations of different kinds of weather.

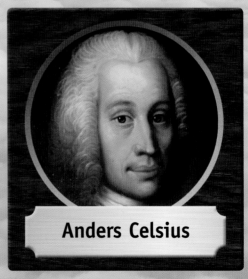

Anders Celsius

Anders Celsius (1701–1744)
Celsius was a Swedish astronomer. He realized that auroras were linked to Earth's magnetic field, and developed the Centigrade, or Celsius, scale to measure temperature.

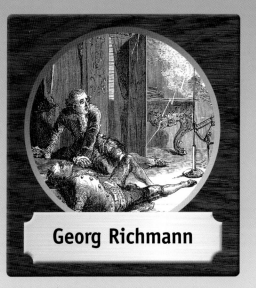

Benjamin Franklin

Benjamin Franklin (1706–1790)
Franklin was an American politician and scientist. His most famous experiment showed that lightning is made of electricity. He invented the lightning rod, or conductor.

Georg Richmann

Georg Richmann (1711–1753)
The German scientist Richmann studied temperature, evaporation, and electric storms. He is said to have been killed by ball lightning.

Alfred Wegener

Alfred Wegener (1880–1930)
German scientist Wegener studied weather at the poles and high in Earth's atmosphere. He was the first to use kites and balloons to collect weather data.

Coching Chu

Coching Chu (1890–1974)
Chinese meteorologist Coching Chu was one of China's leading scientists. He is best known for his work studying typhoons.

James Hansen

James Hansen (born 1941)
American scientist James Hansen is famous for his studies of the atmosphere and climate change, and his campaigning to combat global warming.

Christiana Figueres

Christiana Figueres (born 1956)
Costa Rican diplomat and campaigner Christiana Figueres is a leading United Nations official working in the area of climate change and renewable energy.

GLOSSARY

Aquatic Relating to water.

Broadcast To send out information.

Carbon dioxide A colorless, odorless gas.

Cells An air system created by warm, rising air.

Chemicals Substances made by a chemical process, by nature or by humans.

Condenses The way a gas turns into a liquid when it cools and contracts. Water vapor is a gas that can condense to form liquid water.

Data Information.

Debris The pieces that are left after something has been destroyed—for example, broken branches and fallen trees after a hurricane hits land.

Dehydrated To lose more water than is taken in. It is unhealthy to be too dehydrated.

Equator An imaginary line that runs around Earth halfway between the North Pole and the South Pole.

Evacuated Removed from a place of danger to somewhere that is safe.

Evaporate To change from a liquid into a gas. When liquid water warms up it can evaporate and turn into water vapor—a gas.

Fog A thick cloud of tiny water droplets floating in the air near Earth's surface.

Fossil fuels Fuels such as coal, oil, or natural gas, which are formed from the remains of plants and animals that died millions of years ago.

Friction The force that slows down objects when they slide against each other.

Generator A machine that converts energy from a spinning turbine into electricity.

Geostationary A satellite that seems to remain in the same spot in the sky all the time because it is traveling at exactly the same speed as Earth is rotating below it.

Global warming An increase in the overall temperature of Earth's atmosphere, which many scientists believe is caused mainly by the gases released when humans burn fossil fuels.

Gravity A natural force that pulls all objects in the Universe toward each other. Gravity makes a ball fall toward Earth when a person throws it, and it keeps Earth in orbit around the Sun.

Headlands Narrow areas of land that reach out into the sea.

Heat waves Periods of time when an area experiences unusually high temperatures.

Hemisphere One half of Earth. The Northern Hemisphere is the half north of the equator. The Southern Hemisphere is the half to the south of the equator.

High tides When the water is at its highest level up the coastline.

Humidity The amount of water vapor that is present in the air.

Infrared A type of light ray that cannot be seen by humans, but it can be felt as warmth.

Landslides A natural disaster in which large masses of rocks or earth suddenly and quickly move down the side of a mountain or hill.

Marinas Docks in the sea along the coast where boats can anchor.

Meteorologist A scientist who studies the weather.

Meteors Chunks of rock in space. Meteors that reach Earth's surface are known as meteorites.

Orbit The path one object in space takes around another.

Photovoltaic cells Devices that convert the energy of light into electricity.

Pollution Substances that make things dirty, unsafe, or useless.

Reflected Bounced back.

Renewable energy A type of energy that will not run out because it comes from sources that do not use up natural resources or harm the environment. The Sun, wind, and tides are sources of renewable energy.

Reservoirs Artificial lakes that are built to collect and store water.

Satellite An object in orbit around a planet. People send satellites into space to do work, such as taking photographs of clouds above Earth.

Silt Sand, soil, mud, and tiny pieces of rock that are carried by water and that sink to the bottom of a river, stream, lake, or pond.

Snowdrifts Mounds or hills of snow created by the wind.

Spherical Shaped like a ball.

Temperate Describes regions of the world that usually have warm summer seasons and winters that do not get too cold.

Toxic Poisonous.

Turbine A machine with a set of angled blades that spin around when wind or water push against them.

UFOs Acronym for Unidentified Flying Objects—objects in the sky that some people believe could be spaceships from another planet.

Ultraviolet Rays of sunlight that cannot be seen but that are mainly responsible for sunburn.

Visibility The ability to see or be seen.

Water cycle The movement of water from one form to another in the atmosphere.

Water vapor Water in the form of a gas in the air.

Weather balloons Balloons used to carry weather instruments into the air to measure changes in the atmosphere.

Weather buoys Scientific instruments that collect weather and ocean data on the world's oceans.

INDEX